Luisa Rose
# Don Quixote
## Ausmalbuch für Erwachsene

Bibliografische Information der Deutschen Nationalbibliothek:
Die Deutsche Nationalbibliothek verzeichnet diese Publikation in der Deutschen Nationalbibliografie; detaillierte bibliografische Daten sind im Internet über http://dnb.dnb.de abrufbar.

© 2016 Luisa Rose; 1. Auflage
Covergrafik, Texte & Illustrationen © 2016 Luisa Rose

Herstellung und Verlag: BoD – Books on Demand, Norderstedt

ISBN: 9783743104037

DON QUIXOTE TESTING HIS HELMET

DON QUIXOTE WATCHING HIS ARMOUR

DON QUIXOTE TO THE RESCUE OF ANDREW

THE DESTRUCTION OF DON QUIXOTE'S LIBRARY

DON QUIXOTE AND THE WINDMILLS

DON QUIXOTE AND THE GOATHERDS

THE MANNER OF DON QUIXOTES TRAVEL TO THE INN

HOW SANCHO PAID THE RECKONING

OF THE ADVEN-
TURE OF THE
TWO ARMIES

OF A WONDERFUL ADVENTURE—

THE RICH WINNING OF
THE HELMET OF MAMBRINO

DON QUIXOTE FREES THE GALLEY SLAVES

DON QUIXOTE MEETING CARDENIO

THE STORY OF CARDENIO

DON QUIXOTE DOING PENANCE

THE CURATE & THE BARBER IN DISGUISE.

THE STORY OF
CARDENIO·
·CONTINUED

THE DISCOVERY OF DOROTHEA

THE MEETING OF DOROTHEA & DON QUIXOTE

SANCHO'S STORY OF HIS VISIT TO THE LADY DULCINEA

ANDREW SALUTES DON QUIXOTE

DON QUIXOTE'S EXTRAORDINARY BATTLE

THE ENCHANTMENT OF DON QUIXOTE

THE DISPUTED POMMEL

THE MANNER OF DON QUIXOTE'S RETURN HOME

# Weitere Ausmalbücher von Luisa Rose:

| Titel | ISBN |
|---|---|
| Alice im Wunderland | 9783741297502 |
| Blumen und Märchen | 9783743102002 |
| Der Struwwelpeter | 9783743102699 |
| Die Struwwelliese | 9783743102811 |
| Don Quixote | 9783743104037 |
| Drei kleine Schweine | 9783743104099 |
| Eine Blumenhochzeit | 9783743104105 |
| Fröhliche Reigenspiele | 9783743104112 |
| Lustige Tanzspiele | 9783743104273 |
| Reise ins antike Griechenland | 9783743112568 |
| Flucht ins antike Griechenland | 9783743112599 |
| Pariser Leben im 19.Jahrhundert | 9783743112704 |
| Die Sommerkönigin | 9783743112742 |
| Der Schneider und die Krähe | 9783743112827 |
| Die Wikinger | 9783743113275 |
| Hänsel und Gretel | 9783743114265 |
| Max und Moritz | 9783743103214 |
| Schnurrdirburr | 9783743112834 |
| Mode des 18. und 19. Jahrhunderts | 9783743112971 |
| Kostümbilder des 18. und 19. Jahrhunderts | 9783743114401 |
| Abenteuer im Bienenland | 9783743117051 |
| Griechische Helden der Antike | 9783743117709 |
| Märchen alter Zeit | 9783743116559 |

# Notizbücher von Luisa Rose:

| Titel | ISBN |
|---|---|
| Drachentöter (Notizbuch) | 9783743113077 |
| Natures Wonders (Notizbuch) | 9783743113817 |
| Gedankenspiel Notizen (Notizbuch) | 9783743113886 |
| Smaragd Notizen (Notizbuch) | 9783743114296 |
| Jagd Notizen (Notizbuch) | 9783743114302 |
| Tradition (Notizbuch) | 9783743114319 |
| Antik Notizbuch (Notizbuch) | 9783743114326 |
| Veni Vidi Vici (Notizbuch) | 9783743114340 |
| Black List (Notizbuch) | 9783743114371 |
| Mystic Notes (Notizbuch) | 9783743114388 |
| Magic Notes (Notizbuch) | 9783743114418 |
| Fantasien (Notizbuch) | 9783743114463 |
| Creative Notes (Notizbuch) | 9783743114487 |
| Persönliche Notizen (Notizbuch) | 9783743114494 |
| Peter Pan (Notizbuch) | 9783743114531 |
| Rose (Notizbuch) | 9783743114548 |
| Quality Street (Notizbuch) | 9783743114555 |
| Rubin Notizen (Notizbuch) | 9783743114647 |
| Schmetterlinge (Notizbuch) | 9783743114661 |
| Ali Baba (Notizbuch) | 9783743114678 |
| The portrait of a Lady (Notizbuch) | 9783743114692 |
| Shakespeare (Notizbuch) | 9783743114722 |
| Brainstorming (Notizbuch) | 9783743114739 |
| Merlin (Notizbuch) | 9783743114746 |
| Rügen (Notizbuch) | 9783743114784 |

Möchtest du über neue Bücher von Luisa Rose per email Informiert werden? Dann schicke eine Email mit ‚Newsletter' im Betreff an Luisa.Rose@t-online.de